MY GOOD GRIEF GUIDE

100 Ways To Cope With
Grief When You're Not
A Grown-up

Tara Michener, MA, LPC, NCC

authorHOUSE°

AuthorHouse™
1663 Liberty Drive
Bloomington, IN 47403
www.authorhouse.com
Phone: 833-262-8899

Published by AuthorHouse 07/07/2023

ISBN: 979-8-8230-1125-9 (sc)
ISBN: 979-8-8230-1124-2 (e)

Print information available on the last page.

Dedication

For Duane, Narvell, Lucille (Cealy), Georgia and all of my ancestors that taught me how to grieve.

Affirmations

An affirmation is a statement that you can make that helps you to feel better. You can look in the mirror and say them to yourself, write them in a journal or simply think about them. In this book, I will include affirmations that I made up that you can feel free to use as you need. You can make your own too. Sometimes affirmations can bring us comfort when we need to feel better. They can be things that we believe to be true or things that we need to convince ourselves of.

Affirmation

I don't have to be **strong** for others.

I am worthy when I cry,
when I sigh,
and when I am tired.

I am worthy all on my own.

Note to the Reader

Dear Reader,

When I was in the fifth grade, I learned that I would never see my grandmother again. This did not seem possible. My grandmother had always been there for my family. She was the one that cooked for everybody. Her house was fresh and smelled like home-cooked meals made from scratch. She hosted the holiday dinners. I mean, who was going to make the pies? She picked us up from school when our parents could not. Sleepovers at her house included my safest and happiest memories. I was in my friend's driveway after a long day of play when my mother broke the news to me that my grandmother had died. It was the early evening of March 12th when my mom stood nervously telling me this news, and she looked afraid about what I would do next. I did nothing at first because...I was sure that I heard her wrong. My grandmother could not die; it was impossible. I knew that she was sick, but she had been sick before and was able to go into something called remission. She got well eventually and was up and cooking again, making her house sparkle (because no one cleaned their home as good as my grandma).

But my mom repeated it, "Your grandmother died". The screams that followed those words from my mom were loud and out of control. When I realized they came from my own mouth, I was even more surprised. I noticed that the fence was shaking uncontrollably and saw that my shoe was the one kicking it. My mom grabbed me and was very confused and potentially scared. I was too because a world without my grandmother in it sounded like a scary world. My mom had no idea what to do in that moment. I am sure that it was hard for her to see her daughter unleash yelps and screams on the neighbor's property. I also had no idea what to do. I had never felt so hopeless in my entire life.

Today I am hopeful, and I want to share that with you.

Today I am a therapist, and I am no longer in the fifth grade.

I think about kids that were like me in the fifth grade. Kids hearing the harsh news that their person is no longer alive. I know I needed support and I want to use this book to offer that support to you. I want to do that by offering coping skills. This book won't bring my grandmother or your deceased loved one back, but it will give you 100 ways to get through it…not over it…but through it.

I am giving you what my mom did not have to give me and what I did not know that I needed as a kid. 100 possibilities, opportunities, and coping skills to get through life when experiencing the death of your person.

I hope this helps.

#1 WRITING A LETTER TO YOUR PERSON

One of the things that really bugs me about death is that there are no phone calls. It is final. I love to have the last word but there are no opportunities for those...unless you write them. Writing a letter to your person can be done in a notebook or an index card...you can include it in an active journal or on a piece of notebook paper that you place in an envelope and seal. It is up to you how you would like to make this letter happen...but it helps to make it happen. Writing a letter can help you to get your thoughts out and your emotions, and it gives a person the ability to think about the person that they lost as they communicate. Although it won't bring them back, it gives you a placeholder for all the words that were left unspoken. You don't have to share your letter with others, but you can if you choose. You can read it at a ceremony or bury it under your mattress. What you write and what you do with it is all up to you. It is a coping skill, and it can help.

My cousin died when I was a very young adult, and I was told that she was sick and wanted to see me. I did not get a chance to visit her, and when I was told that she died, I was shocked; I did not think about someone as young as us dying. I quickly grabbed a notebook and told her that I was sorry. I wrote in my messy blue handwriting and told her how much she meant to me, and I told her everything in my head that would fit on the page.

I placed my pen down only after feeling like I said everything that was in my heart. You know what? I did not feel guilty anymore. I did not feel as sad as I did when I got the news…although I was still feeling a lot of pain knowing that I would not see her again, somehow the writing made it easier. I also read it back. When you write your letter, if you choose to keep it, re-reading it can be a helpful tool to make it more real and less shocking.

Another thing that you can try is writing back what you think your person might say if they responded. These are ideas. Make it work for you. Make it your own. There are no right or wrong ways to utilize this coping skill.

<u>A Note for You</u>

In this book... I will refer to the person in your life who died as 'your person'.

I try not to assume that every death that you are processing was a friend, foe or family member. Sometimes people die that are not really that close to you at all, but you still think about them and still need to cope with the absence of them no longer being alive.

Tara

#2 FEELING FACT FINDING

Writing down your feelings can be helpful because death can cause emotions to feel heavy and as overwhelming as a flood. Sometimes it is rough when people ask you to tell them how you feel. You might even want to tell them how you are feeling, but because there are so many feelings, you may not know how to.

Writing down your emotions can give you an understanding and help you to see that it is okay to feel more than one emotion at a time.

You don't have to write them though if you choose to express yourself differently.

You can use paint swatches from a hardware store and tape/glue your emotions by color: anger can be fire engine red and calm can be mint chocolate chip.

It is up to you how you want to express yourself with this activity, but hopefully, working through your emotions in this way gives you a greater sense of relief.

#3 TAKE A BREAK

When someone that you love dies, it can be helpful to take a break.

You get to decide what that break looks like.

You get to decide what that break is from.

You can talk to someone if you need help figuring this one out.

I know that when my dad died, I needed a break from work, and I needed a break from volunteering. I never ever missed meetings before but realized that it was okay because of the circumstances.

It is easy to feel guilty when deciding to take this time for yourself.

Be sure to pay attention to how your emotions show up when you try this one out if you select this as a coping skill to use.

A TEENY TINY FEELINGS LIST

Here is a Brief Feelings List to look at… there are many more emotions than this, but I wanted to get you some examples.

Amused Angry Anxious Ashamed Aggressive Abandoned
Bashful Bored Bubbly Balanced Bitter
Cautious Confused Confident Curious Calm
Disgusted Determined Delighted
Enraged Envious Exhausted Excited Empathic
Frightened Fearful Frustrated
Guilty Grateful Giddy Grumpy
Happy Hurt Humble Hopeful Healing
Isolated Indifferent Impatient
Jealous Joyful Jumpy
Lost Lonely Loved Livid Lucky
Mad Miserable Mean
Nervous Neglected Nostalgic
Overwhelmed Optimistic
Pained Puzzled Protective Peaceful
Regretful Relieved Relaxed Rejected
Silly Sad Sensitive Shocked Shy Sleepy Shamed
Tired Thankful Torn Tense Terrified

#4 SUPPORT SCAVENGER HUNT

Death usually is followed by a lot of people saying they are sorry. They may even say that they are sorry to you. Often you will encounter people asking what you need and feeling sad for you. It is helpful to figure out who you would like to rely on for support. Everyone is not good at all things. If you choose to accept support from someone offering, there is nothing inherently wrong with that. If you need someone to help you with homework for instance but they are not good at the subject, maybe they can help you with something else that fits their talent. It can be hard when experiencing loss to figure out how to tell people exactly what you need because you might feel like you need everything in that moment. Making a list of the people that you are willing to accept help from is a good first step. After you have listed the people, you may want to write a word or two next to them about what they are good at. It helps to assign people tasks that they like or that they enjoy doing. If you are not ready to take support from anyone yet, then that is okay too. You get to decide the terms if you need to ask or accept help. If you don't want to, "no thanks" works just fine. If you don't want to take help from someone now but you might want it later, you can ask the person offering if you can get back with them later. If they say yes, keep that in mind.

Some people like gaining support from others when their person dies, but some find it uncomfortable or awkward. Sometimes when we accept help from others, we can feel like we owe them. If someone is offering support or what is called condolences, there should not be a reason for you to feel like you have to pay them back. It is perfectly normal to accept help, and it is perfectly normal not to accept it at all if you do not want to.

#5 GIVE BACK IN THEIR HONOR

Do you have clothes, food or books that you would like to share with those in need? You can do this in honor of your person, if you choose. You can make your own clothing drive themed by collecting clothing items that your person loved like a tie drive that you can donate to a job enrichment program or a food pantry program with only spaghetti sauce and noodles if your person loved to eat pasta. You can even host a pasta fundraiser dinner in their memory and donate proceeds to a cause that they cared about. An old-fashioned lemonade stand can be a nice way to refresh others and earn money to either donate to a cause your person cared about or to use it to buy something that makes you feel more connected to your person's memory. If you donate books, you can buy labels that mention your person's name and add one to each book so that their memory continues to be associated with something positive that contributes to others.

A Note for You

I watched my aunt step into her kitchen, and she looked different then I was use to seeing her. She wore pajamas, and her face was free of the makeup that she usually wore in abundance. She had a sad look on her face and did not respond the way that I was use to when I was in her kitchen.

You see, my aunt taught me all about fancy hairstyles and makeup. She never looked drab or down; she only ever looked glamourous and even royal. This day she looked very sad. This day I learned about her grief. She told me that this was the day of her daughter's birthday. She had two sons that were much older, but her only daughter had died before I was born. She told me the story of Kelly Deneen, her daughter who died at only two years old. I was given her middle name... Deneen in her honor. She taught me about how stories, names and even grief can be shared.

In that moment, I felt connected to sadness and to a cousin that I would never know. Grief is something that we can feel personally, but we can also feel others' grief.

Have you ever cried while watching a movie, frowned about a sad story or felt down about someone else's misfortune? Grief can connect us even if it is not our own.

— Tara

I OWN my

EMOTIONS.

I can feel
MANY
feelings @ once.

Affirmation

#**6** A FAVORITE THINGS DAY

A favorite things day is a good way to cherish your person's memory by watching shows on TV that they liked, listening to music that they enjoyed or embracing activities that reminded you of your person's life. When my dad died, I planned a day like this on his birthday. It was his first birthday where he would not be able to blow out candles or hear us singing to him. I spent the day enjoying old TV shows that he loved and laughing out loud at comedy that he would have found funny. You can add food and different themes to this day if you want and have it alone or invite others to join you. You don't have to make it a big day. If you choose to keep it simple, it can be one activity that you select such as bike riding or a special place to go like a park that your person enjoyed. Remember this is your grief journey and you are the one that gets to decide what you want to do to cope.

#7 SOMETHING SOFT

It can help to have something soft nearby when grieving. A blanket, a stuffed animal or even a furry pet can bring about an element of comfort. Soft touches can help with sensory processing needs which also helps a lot with grief. Wearing soft sweaters can be a nice way to take the comfort with you, and it allows you to have a wearable coping tool. It can be helpful to visit a craft store that has a multitude of fabrics to sample different textures and nurture the sense of touch. I like silk pillowcases and flannel sheets for bedtime routines. Decide what is best for you.

Affirmation

I **DON'T** accept

Negative comments

about me...
those are

RETURNED

TO SENDER

A Note for You

Did you know that crying can be healthy? It has been said that crying produces the same amount of benefits as chocolate or running a lap.

You may encounter people that tell you not to cry. You may encounter people that tell you that you need to cry.

Your body will hold the answer. We are all different. There is nothing wrong with crying, but there is no need to force yourself to weep.

If you are not able to do it, that is O.K.

-Tara

#**8** YOGA

Yoga is helpful for those that are grieving. Yoga focuses on your breathing, movement and mindset, all things that can be advantageous to do when you're grieving. Don't worry, you don't have to be super flexible or stand on your head. A good yoga practice can simply be inhaling through your nose for four seconds and exhaling from your mouth for four seconds. Touching your toes or simply reaching your arms in the sky can bring relief if you are able to do this. Classes can be a good way to learn more or you can try watching a video online or reading a book that teaches about yoga.

#9 SUPPORT GROUPS

In a support group, various people come together and provide advice, ideas, books and more to assist each other through hard situations. They are built on a promise of trust so that people feel comfortable sharing their thoughts out loud or simply listening to others.

We talked about the process of scavenging your own support that already exists. You can also see if there is a support group with other non-grown-ups in it that have experienced loss. It can be helpful to meet other people who can relate to you and who understand what it is like to grieve. There are many support groups both online and in person that you may want to consider. Some are led by therapists, and some are led by community group non-profits. It is a good idea to find out the training of those helping before joining.

#10 WATER, WATER, WATER

Drink it. Soak in it. Get Sprinkled or splashed.

Drinking water is hydrating which is especially helpful for good health. A grieving person tends to cry a lot which can cause dehydration. Drinking water can also add a sense of calm and allow for processing with the sense of taste. Taking a water break can be helpful to take a moment for yourself. Water also can be helpful with bath soaks, showers, pool dips and beach trips. Running through the sprinkler is not a bad addition to this category either. Jumping in a puddle on a rainy day or watching the waves on a sunny day, many of the five senses can be activated by water.

Affirmation

_I_ can feel _lonely_...

but _I_ am

NOT

alone 😊

A Note for You

Hey there, how are you doing?

I know that this topic can feel heavy, and I wanted to see how you feel about everything that you are reading so far. It is okay to take a moment to try out one of the coping skills and see what you think before continuing to read. If you want to add your own creativity and change something, you can do that too.

– Tala

#11 MEMORY ROCKS

When my dad died, I painted rocks for a lot of people who came to his funeral, and it really helped me. I suggest rock painting because it is easy to find or buy rocks, painting is an activity that helps to reduce stress and you create something that looks nice.

There are many ideas when it comes to rock painting.

You can choose what colors you would like to add to each rock.

The rocks can have words or no words.

Sometimes people add pictures to their art, but you can select what you want to do and maybe even mix it up for variety.

Themes can be fun if you choose your person's favorite band, cereal or something that helps you with memory connection to your person.

#12 CHOOSE A SCHOOL POINT PERSON

It can be hard to have to explain to lots of teachers and staff about your grief. If you have a person that you can connect with your family and your school about your grief on topics ranging from general updates, to how your mood is and everything in between, then this person can help make life less stressful as you cope. Having a person like this in your corner also increases your support network. They can be the main contact for you about the subject, and they can share updates with the rest of the adults in the school that may need them. You might need some help on this one from a grown-up in your life, though. When I was in fifth grade, I was able to tell Mrs. Cross (my media specialist) about my grandma. She not only understood, but she checked on me and was very kind in allowing me extra patience and time when I needed it. Every teacher was not like her and that was okay because she made up for what others did not have. It helps to have at least one grown-up at school who gets it and cares.

I don't have to
convince
people of MY
Light...

Affirmation

They have to shield
their eyes because
of MY

Shine

#13 MAKE A BOUNDARY LIST

You don't have to provide a play-by-play to everyone that you meet but that won't stop people from acting like you should. You can decide who gets specific details and who doesn't. Sometimes people may pressure you to find out more about the way that your person died. It is not your job to keep everyone informed on this, and it can feel bad to be asked at times. Make a list of what you want to share and what you don't want to share. It is okay to tell people you don't want to talk about it when they push too much on aspects you don't want to share about your person.

A Note for You

The first time that I remember going to a funeral, I was confused about the grown-ups that I saw crying. There was a lot of sadness in the room. If you attend an end-of-life event, it can be hard to see those around you acting differently than you are used to. Sometimes people like to share a poem, a story or memory in a program or on a stage with others. Some people like to be with others at events like these so that they feel less alone and more connected to their person.

— Tara

#14 FRESH AIR

Even in the wintertime and in the middle of a blizzard, it can feel good to get some fresh air. There is something about stepping outside and getting fresh air that can give you energy. This helps a lot when you have been in the house or a car a lot. Taking a moment to step outdoors, if you can, for fresh air is a helpful coping skill. Remember the sun is out there and it has Vitamin D.

Affirmation

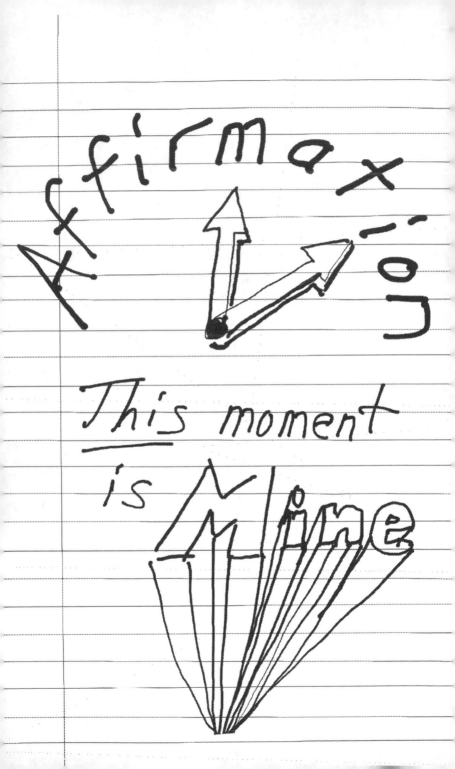

This moment is Mine

#15 JOURNAL

Journaling is a good activity to write down what you are thinking. There are so many ways you can use it. You can write about your day. You can write your thoughts. You can also make short stories, poetry or keep it as a memory log. Journals preserve your inner thoughts, and it helps to get the words out of your head and onto paper.

#16 GRATITUDE LISTS

When you are in grief, it can be tough to see the good things. Gratitude lists can help to provide proof of the things that help to clarify a sense of thankfulness. You can choose one thing that you are grateful for each day and just think about it. You can draw your list or write it. If you want, you can share your list with someone that you know and ask them about their list. Your list can be about anything you choose. You can even center it around your person if you want by writing about what you are grateful for about their life and memory.

I don't have to understand everything because I am still learning.

I AM a good learner.

Affirmation

#**17** PICTURES

Draw pictures of you and your person. Sketch the things that make you think of them. Take photos with a camera or your phone of things that you would have sent to your person. Put them in a book if you want or organize them in a frame or on a wall. Scrapbook with the photos that you already might have of them when they were alive.

#18 MEMORY BOARD

Make a memory board using old magazine pictures, glue and other craft materials. Include pages of things that you liked to do together and what made your relationship the way that it was. Add things that you want to do to keep their memory active and fresh.

A Note for You

I am wondering if it is annoying to you when people say they know how you feel? It can be tough because how can they know... when you might not know?

I liked when people asked how I felt more than I liked them telling me that they know. There is something about asking a question that can feel better than making a statement.

How do you feel about this? What do you want to hear?

— Tara

#**19** ENJOY NATURE

Get outside and listen to the birds sing, the crickets chirp and watch the leaves of the trees sway. Nature reminds us that beauty is all around us. The colors, sounds and atmosphere can be interesting to watch and an inspiration for your next painting or an item on your gratitude list.

Affirmation

I believe
in my
ability to

Heal

#**20** MAKE A 'JUST IN CASE' SENSORY TOOL BOX

Add items from all the five senses. Things that you can taste like peppermint candy or gum. Things that you enjoy looking at like photos, beautiful rocks, etc. Things that you can hear like a shaker full of shells or marbles. Things that you can smell like a sachet or perfume or a cologne card, etc. Things that you can feel like a soft piece of cloth or silk.

Add these items to a box that you can easily get to when you need a 'pick me up'.

Affirmation

Even in a croweded space...

← ME

I stand out and make it Better.

#21 MAKE
AFFIRMATION CARDS

You are familiar with affirmations, right? They are all throughout this book. A quick recap...affirmations are statements that affirm your worth, being and sense of purpose. Write about your strengths and add them to cards. You can choose colorful cards that are fancy or simply use an index card or notebook page. It is more about what you write than what you write it on.

#22 CONSIDER A HUG

You get to choose who touches you and who you touch. If you have someone in your life that you trust and you feel like a hug from them is helpful, ask them for a hug. A healthy and kind hug from a trusted and safe person can ease stress. Remember you do not have to hug someone that you do not want to hug…this is also self-care.

Affirmation

- - - - - - - - - - - - -

My joy can exist
even on days
that I cry.

#**23** GET SLEEP

I know that the last thing that you need is another grown-up telling you to go to sleep. It can be hard to actually remember to go to bed when you are feeling stressed about loss. Try to make sure that you are getting enough sleep to give you the energy that you need to get closer to healing. I promise that I am not trying to nag on this one. If you cannot sleep once you are in bed, sometimes it helps to just lie down and rest.

A Note for You

Many changes happen when our person dies. When things change, it can feel scary or odd. Some people even notice that they have a different appetite or do not want to do the things that they liked as much as they did before.

You might want things to change, or you might want things to stay the same and enjoy routines.

—Tara

#**24** USE POSITIVE SELF-TALK

It can be easy to say negative things to yourself when you are grieving. Remember to say nice things to yourself even when you don't want to. Remind yourself that you are doing the best that you can. Give yourself the benefit of the doubt and forgive yourself for mistakes and missteps.

#25 DANCE PARTY

Movement helps! You don't have to be good at it but just move as much as you choose. Play your favorite music and allow yourself the opportunity to enjoy it. Bopping your head only is fine too. You can bring others into the fun or simply dance alone. Dancing it out can increase positive emotions.

#26 BLOW BUBBLES

A bubble machine or actually blowing bubbles is nice to add to a coping skills list. A machine gives a sense of party and fun. Blowing bubbles helps you to catch your breath and actively create a break for joy. Bubbles are easy to pack and can also help to bring forth feelings of peace and serenity.

#27 CLAY AND PLAY

Clay is nice to use to be active with your hands. Sculpt or simply immerse yourself into the sensory aspect that clay provides. Choose different colors that you enjoy. Make something special for someone else or keep it just for you.

Affirmation

I am _Thankful_
for my abilities.

#28 PLAY AN INSTRUMENT

If you play an instrument already, this is a good time to play it even more. If you are interested in trying out an instrument or choosing a new instrument to play, you can do that. Music can be very soothing and allow for calm and peace.

#29 MOVIE DAYS

Movies can be helpful especially movies where loss happens. This can be hard to watch sometimes, but for some people, they feel like it helps them to relate to their own loss and to feel less alone. Although it is still hard for me, I enjoy watching movies where there is a loss of a dad because I can relate to that, and it makes me feel a sense of belonging.

My grief is my own
and its O.K. if it looks
different than
someone ele's grief.
I don't have to be like
everyone else ...

I can be myself
AND
still grieve.

AFFIRMATION

#**30** COLORING BOOKS

There are a lot of coloring books to choose from that have a broad range of designs and themes. Sometimes using a colored pencil or a crayon can really decrease anxious feelings. You don't have to color inside of the lines or outside of the lines, just do it the way that you want; this is your space to color and you get to make it the way you want.

#**31** STRESS BALL

You can buy a stress ball or make your own by taking balloons and filling them with items like rice or sand. Stress balls help to ease discomfort and bring a sense of calm.

#**32** GRIEF GAME NIGHT

Games help so much to create connection. Think about someone in your life that might want to have a game day or night with you. It helps if this person knows your person that died. It can be a bonding experience. You can name it after your person. You can have it on a regular basis or just once in a while.

#**33** MAKE A TIMELINE

You can make a timeline of milestones that matter to you involving your person. You can do this in a notebook, on a large sheet of paper or any way that works for you. It helps to start with the special memories that you will miss with your person as well as things that have become routine that will change because your person is no longer alive. This is something that you can do with a partner or alone.

✷ Affirmation ✷

I can use my thoughts to problem-solve

#34 HAVE A SENSORY FOOD DAY

You can ask your grown-up, for example, if you can have a salty breakfast, a spicy lunch and a sweet and sour dinner. This can be enjoyable, but it also helps your sensory experience. It can be a tasty way to bring variety and a bit of fun into your day as you work towards coping.

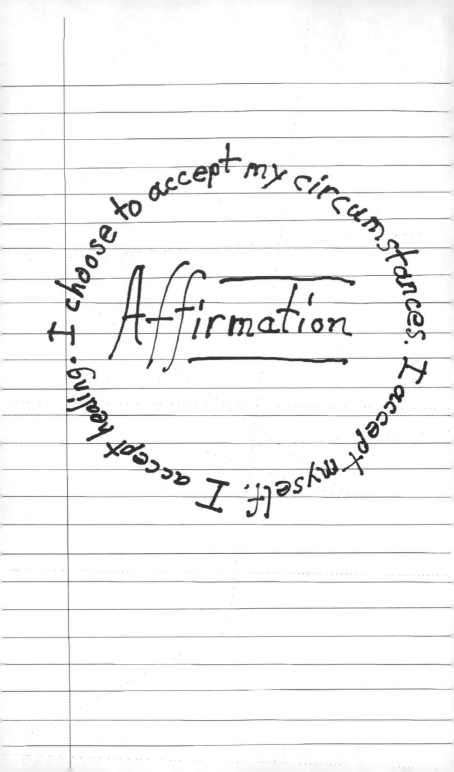

Affirmation

I choose to accept my circumstances. I accept myself. I accept healing.

#35 MAKE AN EMOJI METER

Use Emojis to rate your morning, afternoon, and night, adding colors to your creation too, if you want. This can help to keep your own visual record of how you feel.

#**36** SOLVE A PUZZLE

Did you know solving a puzzle is also solving a problem? When you can do this, it can create better pathways to problem-solving. Crosswords, word searches, Sudoku, there are so many puzzles you can choose from! You can even start collecting puzzles to give yourself more variety.

#37 PLAY IN THE SAND

You can do a lot with this one. Kinetic sand, a trip to the beach, moon sand, or any kind of activity that involves dirt or sand works here. A lot of people find that gardening or plant work can also fit this category. If you choose to nurture your own garden, you can dedicate it to your person and name it after them if you choose. It can feel healthy to take care of living things when someone that you know dies. Sometimes people gift your family plants when you are dealing with loss. You can ask if you can help take care of these plant gifts if you want.

⇒ Affirmation ⇐

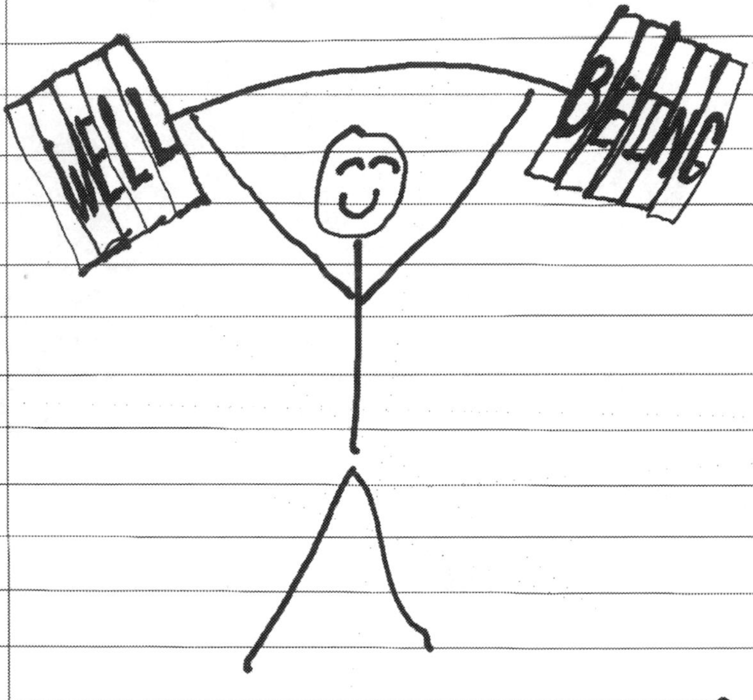

I am dedicated to my....

#**38** WRITE A SPEECH

You can write a speech and you don't have to recite it unless you want to. Writing a speech about your person can give them a special place of attention in a report, at a ceremony or just for you to acknowledge how much they mean to you.

A Note for You

How do you feel about your person?

This can be a very tough subject. When my dad died, I hoped to be able to have an option to say 'yes' or 'no' to some of his belongings that had sentimental value. However, I was not able to get access to these things, although a lot of my siblings did.

Some people don't want their person's possessions however some people do. For some, they hold on to things for a long time and others donate items right away (which is what happened in my situation). It can be hard if you feel like you don't have any say in how things that your person owned get handled after they die.

— Tara

#**39** FACT FINDING INTERVIEWS

An activity that some people like to do for coping and memory making is finding people who knew their person and interviewing them about their person's life. This is an interesting exercise because it is from the viewpoint of someone else other than yourself. It can feel like meeting your person all over again when you gain someone else's thoughts about them.

You might want to ask questions like "How did you meet?", "What is your favorite memory?" and any other questions you find suitable.

I am
Complete,

Affir-
ma--tion

Even when
I am missing
Someone I ♡.

#**40** LEARN A NEW HOBBY

What have you always wanted to try, but haven't yet? This may be the time. Choose a new hobby and see how that goes. Learning something new helps our brain focus and can be a welcome deviation when things are hard.

#**41** MAKE A COMPLIMENT BOARD

What do people usually like about you? Write it down. When you hear something nice about yourself, preserve it. Draw pictures or write them out. When you need to feel better, this is a handy thing to have around to show you what people in your life think about you. No more shrugging off compliments. Embrace them. Save them.

#**42** TAKE A MINI VACATION

Grab a beach blanket, books, and your favorite snacks and eat outside. Imagine yourself on your dream vacation. Close your eyes and visualize where you would like to go and who you would like to be with you. Your imagination is important and worth preserving. You deserve time to get away even if it is a small break on a blanket; it is yours and you can decide what you want to do.

Affirmation

I can

think of ideas to
make me feel
better when I need to.

<u>A Note, for YOU</u>

So much might be going on around you that you might not have sayin. You may not be able to choose arrangements about your person or even have a say in decisions that grown-ups around you make, but you are still important, even if you don't feel like you have a say. When life changing things happen because someone that you love dies, it can be very tough. I want you to know that even if your opinion is not used, it still matters and counts.

— Tara

#**43** TAKE A HIKE

We talked about nature and how it can be helpful. A nature hike can give you the benefits of the outdoors paired with exercise. At the beginning of the hike, you might feel a sense of challenge, and at the end, a sense of accomplishment. In between is the real treat though, stop and look around at all of the creatures and wildlife around you.

Affirmation

I am

NOT

responsible

for bad

things that

happen.

#44 REFRAME

I am not talking about pictures when I say reframe...I am talking about your thoughts. If you start with a negative thought, visualize a large stop sign bigger than a large plate, imagine the word stop, and after it, visualize your first name. Then restart your thought without the negativity. For example, I am not smart (visualize the stop sign with your name); reframe: I am smart, I just need help with this.

#45 BUILD SOMETHING

A tower, a skyscraper or anything you choose can be built with Legos, blocks or any item that you see fit. Stacking items on top of each other to create a structure can be fun and add to a sense of accomplishment. Jenga is a good example of this in game form. You can do this with a partner or alone.

#46 RETELL STORIES ABOUT YOUR PERSON

I find that people love telling stories about their person. I think it helps to keep their memory alive and can kind of introduce them to new people by sharing a funny thing that they did or used to do. I enjoy telling stories about my dad kind of like this:

> "My dad had a very big sweet tooth. One day my brother and I saw him eating marshmallows in a bowl with milk… really I am not kidding! My brother asked him about it, and he claimed they were diet marshmallows! We did not believe him and were pretty sure that diet marshmallows did not exist, but it was a good try for him to keep that bowl in his hands. It did not work. My brother swiftly took the sweet treat away from my

dad and told him he needed to watch his sugar level!"

Everyone that I tell that story to usually laughs at my dad's childlike desire for sugar and I enjoy seeing how my dad can still make people laugh even though he is no longer alive. What stories would you share if you chose this coping skill?

A Note for You

Are you angry at your person?

Sometimes we feel mad at our person for leaving. Sometimes we feel guilty about feeling mad. And sometimes we feel all of these emotions at the same time. It is normal to feel a variety of ways about your person emotionally.

—Tara

Affirmation

OUT

IN

I can control
my
breathing

#**47** CAMPING

Camping or simply sitting around a fire or fireplace can be soothing. Fire is pretty to look at but please be sure to have a grown-up near you if you are roasting a marshmallow or hot dog for the best safety results. You can tell stories around a campfire or simply just enjoy the colorful flicker of the flames and the crackle of the fire.

A Note for You

Do you find yourself replaying circumstances of your person's life over and over again?

This is common. I still replay moments from my life with my grandma. I think about the last Christmas that I had with her. She was really sick, and I remember thinking I could not wait until she gained weight again. I longed for the next holiday when she would be back in her kitchen cooking for us instead of lying on her mother's couch being served and cared for. She did not get to go shopping that year, so she gave us the rare gift of money. I replay that scene

so much, but now I
think, "what was she thinking
that day?" Did she know
that she would miss my
promotion to sixth grade?
    What about you? Do
you replay scenes?
Write them down if you
want; it might help in
processing them.

                    ~ Tara

#48 DECORATE CUPCAKES, COOKIES OR OTHER SWEET TREATS

If you can grab lots of frostings, sprinkles and decorations, you can be a mini bake shop. Top your treats the way that you like; it can feel stress-reducing to beautify your baked goods. Share them with someone who you think would enjoy them.

A Note for You

Some people can find it hard to have fun when their person is no longer alive. Your joy is not a bad thing to your person. Your joy helps you to cope and your coping helps you to make the most of your life.

    —Tara

#**49** HAVE A MANTRA

Repeat encouraging truths over and over again. For example, you can say, "I am loved." When you say things like this, when you feel like you need it, the words really help.

#**50** SIDEWALK CHALK MURALS

Find a sidewalk that you can top with drawings, sketches and all the colors of chalk that you enjoy. Make it yours and mark it up just the way that you like it.

A Note for You

It can be very hard when grief hits you out of the blue, and all of a sudden, you feel the need to cry or to react... especially in public. I can say that this can be part of the grieving process. It is not odd that you feel this way, although it may feel involuntary. It may be your body's way of giving itself what it needs. Everybody may not understand this, but sometimes the only person that needs to get it is you.

— Tara

#51 PICK FLOWERS OR FRUIT

Take some time to smell the roses and pick a few while you are at it. There are fields and spaces where you can pick wildflowers, berries, apples and all kinds of cool things. It is fun and the one time where you get to be picky, and it is okay. Just don't pick these items in someone's private yard.

#**52** MAKE A SOUNDTRACK

Think of all your favorite songs and remix them, reel them or write out the lyrics. Enjoy them.

#53 WIGGLE YOUR FINGERS AND YOUR TOES

I know that one might sound weird but trust me (or don't) but wiggling your fingers and your toes at the same time feels like stress relief. Write about it after you do it. Give yourself at least a minute or two for this exercise.

A Note for You

When your person dies, it never fails that people will tell you about their person. I have done that myself, right? It seems that the grief experience is so universal that sharing can bring comfort so be aware that you may hear many more stories, ones that you ask for and ones that you don't, both from people that you know and from strangers too.

— Tara

#54 BUILD A BLANKET FORT

Indoor forts can be fun. Make it a special space for calming or adventure. Forts are nice for reading, napping or just taking a moment for yourself.

#55 FLY A KITE

Take some time to let yourself soar (or at least let your kite soar).

#56 LOOK FOR SHAPES IN THE CLOUDS

Cloud watching can be a lot of fun. Take some time to figure out what you see when you look up. This can be enjoyed alone or with others.

#**57** STAR GAZING

If you are able to stay up late enough, look up and try to catch a view of the stars. A telescope helps tremendously with this activity.

#**58** MAKE A WISH LIST OF WHAT YOU WANT TO DO IN FIVE YEARS

Thinking about the future can be a positive way to appreciate what is next. What do you want to accomplish? Where do you want to go? What do you want to do? Ask yourself questions like this. Making a list of who you want to be in five years can be a worthwhile activity.

#**59** MAKE AND FLY PAPER AIRPLANES

Make and fly paper airplanes, even race them. You can decorate your planes and make them in all sizes and colors.

#60 HAVE BREAKFAST FOR DINNER

Pancakes, syrup and all the fixings can make a nice breakfast bar for dinner. It can be fun to enjoy the sense of taste to bring your mood up and apply creativity to your table.

A Note for You

When your person dies, some people can experience an emotion called denial.

Denial, when it comes to grief, means not really believing that your person is dead. It can feel like the person is still alive. Some people accidentally call their person's phone number expecting an answer from them.

It can be challenging to have to remind yourself often that your person is no longer alive.

— Tara

#61 PLACE A DREAM NOTEBOOK UNDER YOUR PILLOW

Your person might be in your dreams when you go to sleep. When you have dreams, there might be details that you want to remember, but often dreams can be forgotten easily. A notebook close by can be a handy tool to record your dreams and recall what happens in your dreams so that you can remember them better.

#**62** MAKE A FIDGET BOX

Pieces of pool noodles, toy nuts and bolts, pom poms, monkey noodles, fidget spinners and pipe cleaners are all great fidget items that utilize your hands and sense of touch. You collect these items and put them in a container to make your own fidget box. Then you can use the items inside your box to help you to calm down and ease anxious thoughts.

Affirmation

I am a good

Friend

#63 ENJOY A WEIGHTED BLANKET

Weighted blankets are soothing and calming. They have been known to ease anxious thoughts as well.

#**64** WATCH THE SUNSET AND THE SUNRISE

It can be soothing to see the different color schemes that appear in the sky during sunset and sunrise. You can make this a regular part of your routine and couple it with another coping skill like affirmations or prayer.

#65 GET NATURAL LIGHT

Open the blinds, pull back the curtains and let natural light in. It helps to brighten your day, literally.

#**66** GO TO A MUSEUM

Museums come in all varieties. You can make a list of local attractions as well as those that are further away. Getting immersed in exhibits and displays can be a perfect way to spend a day coping in a healthy way.

Affirmation:

I can

Reflect

when I want

to embrace

favorite

memories.

A Note for You

Sometimes it may seem that everyone else has forgotten about your person because they create new relationships and connections and talk less about the person that you lost. This can spur many different feelings.

If you are struggling with thinking that no one else cares about your person it may be helpful to think about how you feel like your person should be regarded and see if it is something you can get others excited about. I realize there are no guarantees, but death is an interesting occurrence where people handle it in different ways and some may appear to drift away from your person.

— Tara

#67 ASSIGN AN ACCOUNTABILITY COACH

Find someone in your life to make sure that you are doing what you need to. Write down a list that they should ask you about. It can be advantageous to have a supportive person that you trust to keep you on track.

#**68** DOODLE

This one is nice because you don't need a fancy crayon or sharpie; a pencil works just fine. Doodling can be done with any paper or writing utensil. You don't need a fancy notebook either (unless you want one).

#**69** TIDY UP

Yes, I said it…clean your room. Don't get me wrong this can be fun! Really, it can. Decorate, throw away old clutter and add some new touches. It can be refreshing to have a whole new space to call your own.

#**70** QUOTE SHOP

Find a bunch of quotes and save the ones that you like.
Write them in your journal, add them to a frame or share
them in a card with someone else.

#**71** WRITE AND DRAW
A COMIC STRIP

You get to decide who the main character is! You can absolutely use situations from your life and reframe them into comedy or action segments; it's your story to write!

A Note for You

When my dad died, I did not know what to do with myself. There would be times where I felt like I needed to just do something, but I had no idea where to start. This is one of the reasons why I wrote this book for you! I want to give you many things to do if you choose to. I noticed that I felt better when I could use the energy that I had on things that I wanted to.

Tara

#**72** READ A JOKE BOOK

If you don't own a joke book you can check one out at the library. Laughing is good for you.

#73 MAKE A LIST OF JOURNAL PROMPT IDEAS... AND USE THEM!

Once you have a journal, it is a good idea to know what to put in it. Gather journal prompt ideas and use them as you are able to.

#**74** LEARN A NEW LANGUAGE

There are a lot of ways to learn a language that you don't know. You can get a book, use a computer program or take a class.

#**75** GO BOWLING

Bowling is a fun activity and a sport! You can join a league or go occasionally.

Affirmation

I am worthy
of good

Friends.

#**76** ENTER A PINEWOOD DERBY RACE

There are many of these races all over. You can look up ones in your area and construct your own vehicle.

#**77** PLAY THE FLOOR IS LAVA

This can be fun in a small space or a larger one with others.

#**78** MAKE A NO-SEW BLANKET

Get fabric, scissors and maybe a bit of help. You can keep it for yourself, share it or donate it to someone.

#**79** JUMP ROPE

Jumping rope can be fun and great exercise. It helps to work up a sweat and this can be helpful to ease sadness and reduce stress.

#80 BASKETBALL

Basketball can be fun whether playing pickup games with others or simply shooting hoops alone. You can also practice drills like catching, passing and dribbling.

Affirmation

I can set
health boundaries

A Note for You

   It may be tempting to feel like you want to bargain at times to bring back your person. Many people have thoughts like, "if I could only see them again ... I would do [insert bargain]".
This is a natural part of the grieving stage, but it is also not up to you to feel responsible for your person being here or not.
That can be a lot of pressure to put on yourself.
It is not your fault.
No matter what.
It is not your fault.

                    —Tara

#**81** MAKE A BIRD FEEDER:

Nurturing animals can feel nurturing to us. You can ask someone to join you to make feeders for gifts or simply make one on your own for the birds in your area.

#82 VISIT A BUTTERFLY GARDEN

Find a local one or ask if this is something that you might be able to do on a trip. Sometimes you can even look into education kits or do-it-yourself articles where you might be able to make your own with some help.

#**83** HAVE A CARTOON MARATHON

Find all the cartoons that you enjoy and watch a bunch of them. You can have your favorite snacks handy and even invite someone else to watch with you.

#**84** COLLECT CARDS

There are so many different types of card decks that you can collect. Do you enjoy a sport or activity? See if they have collectible cards and keep them stored in a nice book or box.

Affirmation

I am a
__balanced__
person

#**85** READ THE CHILDREN'S BOOKS THAT YOU LOVE THE MOST

You can select books from when you were younger or current ones...or both. Children's books hold so many memories and insights for us.

A Note for You

Do you ever feel like maybe your loss is not on the same level as someone else's?

You are reading this book, so you are able to grieve just like anyone else. It is not a competition. I used to feel bad grieving about my grandma when I was around someone who lost a parent. It is not my job or their job to decide whose loss is more significant. Every loss is significant.

— Tara

#86 MAKE JEWELRY

Get some beads, gems or something else and put it all together. It can feel relaxing to take some time to create something that you can wear.

#87 DRINK
SOMETHING WARM

Hot cider, tea or cocoa can be very soothing and calming
and feed the sensory need of taste.

#**88** MAKE A FIST
AND THEN RELAX

Making a tight fist and then relaxing it can ease tension and help you to feel calmer.

#**89** MAKE SELF-LOVE NOTES AND SAVE THEM FOR WHEN YOU NEED THEM

Write love notes to yourself and when you feel like you need kindness…open one up.

GOAL!

noitamriffA

I ¼ can set good goals for my Happiness

#90 HAVE A RANDOM ACTS OF KINDNESS DAY

Decide if you want to pick up trash in a park or neighborhood, hand out flowers, or something else...but be random and be kind.

A Note for You

Depression is something that you might hear often in regard to grief. Most people feel very sad when their person dies. Feelings of depression is not the same thing as clinical depression. At times, the sadness can be overwhelming though. It can be hard to do the things that you used to easily do. It is a part of the process of loss.

— Tara

#91 TIE DYE A SHIRT

You can learn online or grab a kit from a store. Use an old T-shirt and gift it to someone else or keep it for yourself or both.

#92 MAKE YOUR OWN NEWSLETTER FOR PEOPLE IN YOUR LIFE OR JUST FOR YOU

Make a newsletter and include new things happening in your week, month or year. Share it online or print it and send it to friends and family who may not live as close.

#93 SCREAM

Yep. Scream. This one you might want to warn your grown-ups about first so they know that you are okay. After you have warned them…do it!

#94 MAKE A CALMING JAR OR BOTTLE

Your grown-ups might not like me after this, but you will need glitter…probably a lot of it. These jars or bottles can be so helpful to focus and find peace.

#**95** PRACTICE A RESPONSE

Did someone say something to you that you do not know how to reply to? Think of what you'd want to say next time. Practice it. Write it down. Think about it. Rehearse it.

#96 SAY THANK YOU

You can do this with cards, calls, notes or in any way you choose, but if someone has done something nice for you, take some time to acknowledge them in your own way.

#**97** WRITE DOWN THE PROS AND CONS OF YOUR CHOICES

Sometimes it is not clear what is right or wrong so write it down. What is good about things in your life and what might not be as good? Take some time to use this model to help you to make decisions that you feel confident about.

#98 ASK YOUR GROWN UP ABOUT THERAPY

It might be helpful to understand what therapy is and if it is right for you. This can usually be answered by talking to someone that you trust and asking them for help to learn more.

Affirmation

I can make
decisions that
make me feel better
emotionally.

#99 MAKE SLIME

Slime is really good for the sensory need of touch. There are many recipes, but if you want to, you can always buy it.

#**100** WRITE YOUR THOUGHTS ABOUT HOW YOU WILL USE THIS BOOK

This book can be used over and over again, or you can read it once and share it with someone else who might need it. Take some time to journal your thoughts and think about what coping means to you.

Final Note from Tara

I am so glad that you chose to read this book. When I was a kid, I felt like anytime something like death was brought up, the subject changed, but then people that I loved and needed died. I did not have answers on how to carry on life with my person(s) no longer living. I learned that when some people die, I would have to get used to a new way of living. Sometimes this was in small ways like the person who always liked my jokes would no longer be able to laugh at them. Then it was in larger ways like missed milestone parties and celebrations like graduation, weddings and more. I learned that, as long as I could preserve the memories, the loss was not permanent, but it would never be the same as it was before. I needed to cope. This is why you are reading this note from me now...I know that you may need to cope too, but it is hard to think about what you need when you are grieving. Some of these ideas will be your favorite things to try when you open this book and some of them you may never try at all. You might make some of them altered in a way that fits your life more and some of them you may use just as they are written. There is no judgement here…only support. I hope this book helps you and is a welcome reminder that, as I wrote this book, I thought about you. One of the hardest aspects of loss can be feeling lonely, and if I can help make you feel a little bit less alone…that works for me. Acceptance is a word that many associate with loss. It can take a while to get to that point. Everyone is different. Everyone is unique. Everyone experiences loss. I am sure that everyone will want you to follow a process that they think is right but you are you…and your process may look like the best way for you to cope. I gave you 100 ways to cope with loss. I hope that you know these are tools and not expectations for you to get over it. I do hope that they help you to get closer to healing and to get through it. Good grief is defined by you. So one last coping skill for you…I know that I said 100 but this is a bonus… Define what good grief is for you. Not for others…but for you. This definition might change every day and that is okay…keep defining it for yourself. Some days it might be throwing a ball and other days it might be throwing a fit. I wish you good grief on your own terms.

Printed in the United States
by Baker & Taylor Publisher Services